The Alphabet of Women

The Alphabet of Women

Edited by
Miriam Hechtman

For
Patti, Audre, Sylvia, Carol Ann, June, Mary, Joan, Emily, Joy,
Maya, Evelyn, Sappho, Gertrude, Kae, Dorothy, Lucille,
Wislawa, Ali, Oodgeroo, Charlotte, Naomi, Layli, Toni,
Anais, Hildegard, Virginia

Always
For my mother, my grandmothers and my sisters,
and for my daughters Noa + Lina

The Alphabet of Women
ISBN 978 1 76109 228 2
Copyright © individual contributors 2022
Copyright © this collection Miriam Hechtman 2022
Cover: Grace Felstead

First published 2022 by
Ginninderra Press
PO Box 3461 Port Adelaide 5015
www.ginninderrapress.com.au

Contents

Foreword		7
Introduction		9
Atlas	Anna Forsyth	11
Ballet	Bina Hammer	13
Canvas	Amanda Cohen	15
Desire	Daiane Moret	17
Exceptional	Erica Hacker	19
Frankincense	Tanya Southey	22
Girl Guidelines	Gabrielle Journey Jones	24
HA	Janette Hoppe	25
I	Anne Casey	28
Jewgirl Juju	Joanne Fedler	30
Plosives and Explosives Are Coded in Its Sound	Devika Brendon	34
Lullaby	Ruth Fesseha	38
M for Marie (who'd prefer to be N for naughty and nude)	Marie McMillan	40
The New Nude	Stacey Cotter Manière	43
Who showed you how to feel good?	Rowan Rose	45
Dear Letter P	Miriam Hechtman	46
Quick to quote me as queen	Boy Renaissance	48
Eternally Persistent	Andrijana Miler	49
Sound	Sarah Temporal	50
Tuesday's Still Life	Ginette Ball	52
Uterus	Rana Salem	54
To the Earth, Love V	Vanessa S. Lee-AhMat	57
Women's Eyes	Ella Mitchell	58
Ex Tempore	Lou Steer	59
I Used To Ask Y	Jessica Chapnik Kahn	61
Layers of Z	Limor Fayena	62

About the Authors	65
Acknowledgements	72

Foreword

I happen to be a poetry lover but it's been a long time.

I am reminded as I read this collection of that longed-for transportation which great poetry can deliver.

I sit and as I read, my numb and mildly upset experience is changed into something more delicate and rich.

These poems are a surprise present to me.

Sometimes, poetry can put into words the things we know are there but could not ourselves find a way to say. Other times, poetry puts into words things you didn't know were there but feel familiar and true.

Great poems, such as those in this collection, do both.

Ione Skye

Introduction

The Alphabet of Women was accidentally conceived at sunrise, back in March 2018, as I lay awkwardly horizontal at the bottom of my bed while my young daughters slept. The night before had been fretful. Both had been ill and I had been in and out of sleep attending to their needs through those small hours. It was also the morning of Poetica's first International Women's Day gathering and I had not written a word to mark the day.

So I lay there. Still as a mother who doesn't want to wake her children, my phone in hand, notes open, and I began typing in words. Patriarchy. Patriotism. Policing. Whispering the words with gravitas. And I soon realised that the letter P had a lot of explaining to do. In a *Sesame Street* sort of way. But for adults. 'Dear Letter P,' I began, 'you have let us down.' And so began my ode to the letter P. It felt a little absurd 'oding' to the letter P but blaming the letter felt somewhat symbolic of having no one to blame in a system that has done a disservice to us all.

I performed the poem that night to a very enthusiastic audience and a friend casually suggested I write the whole alphabet. I laughed. Thought, 'no way'. But a seed had been planted. And seeds have a tendency to grow especially in budding poets.

Fast forward to May 2019 and the title *The Alphabet of Women* landed in my notes. After much contemplation, I decided the best way to tell the story of woman was to share the alphabet with twenty-five other 'women' poets. Diversity and representation was paramount in telling the whole and real story of woman and letters were allocated with this in mind. Poets were challenged twofold – the anthology would be both a womanhood inquiry but also a poetic challenge using alliteration as the key. The letter was key to the words. The story was open. Poems could be anything related to women, woman, but had to incorporate words with the allocated letter. Themes around women could vary as could style. From rage to tenderness, politics to the body, motherhood to daughterhood to sisterhood to vaginas to mother earth, poets were invited to follow their heart.

So here they are: *The Alphabet of Women*.

Miriam Hechtman

Atlas

1.

She who holds the world
on her shoulders
mother Atlas, by name
to uphold, support
enduring Atlas
the celestial axis
on which all children
revolve.

2.

Atlas as the mountain range
Divine Feminine
only lofty to the weary
it's lonely at the top
waiting for the one
the pilgrim
willing to suffer altitude sickness
to break the spell.

3.

Feminism is the original
astronomer
Atlas extending her reach
creating lenses
mapping the heavens
capturing the infinite
possibilities

4.

The geography evolves
women wait
for the new cartographers
the brave retellers
of her-story
their bodies
futures
on the line.

Anna Forsyth

Ballet

Before I boldly bantered
With a bronze-eyed boy
On a bus after seeing you
Then brazen, burrowed
For his number

Before I asked a girl
With bendy hair who
Bubbled with stars to my bed
Then whispered in her ear
Everything besides kisses

Before I blushed at a
Builder's smile then
Bent closer than I should
Buttoned myself to her
Sooner than I should

Before I told you
About each of these ballets
Away and watched the
Whole seep from your
Broad brave shoulders

Before that there was
This – a beginning
Where we ate braided bread
And baked and boiled stories
From each other

A beginning, where I
Bundled into you on a
Bench on Burton Street
And beneath my cheek
Felt the balm of your belief

A beginning, before
I knew
How much I'd bite away
From your breath to
Feed mine

And here
I am,
Ravenous,
Still so
Ravenous.

Bina Hammer

Canvas

I was cultivated in a cultural curriculum on my curves –
which to covet, which to cover, which convert to currency
 or cause blood to course through capillaries like electrical currents.
  How captivating I could be
   tracing fingers delicately over concaving clavicles,
    swirling my hips to curl like calligraphy.
     Chiselling my crooked edges,
      confining them to clean lines like crisp white shirt collars.
       Waltzing classical cafeteria choreography:
        Count calories. Cut carbs. Curb cravings.
         Colloquialisms coined 'cankles' and 'cottage cheese thighs'
          and confiscated my confections –
           replaced with cosmetic collections to complement my complexion.
            My face, a creamy canvas for colouring, for contouring,
             to be crafted like the cupcake created to sparkle
              and be captured on camera, but not consumed.
             For cascading hues. For catching the light.
             For cat eyes and casting come-hither glances.
             My attributes calibrated and catalogued –
              which to claim as character, which to camouflage.
            Which critical combinations convey that cool, candy-coated cachet.
           Commit my skin to coverage creams to correct and conceal,
          caulking creases like leaky sinks.
        Coached to pose for casual conversation
        cajoling the corners of my mouth into their crowd-pleasing crescent formation.
       For charisma and compliments, well-timed clever comments.
      I was cautioned against a lady's excessive conveyance of confidence,
     given its link to our counterpart's castration.
   Carnality is a poetic curation –
a cave of crimson rivers, a cavern for quivering climaxes –

charged to demonstrate containment.
 Keep it clothed and crested,
   cloaked and candescent,
   cool, calm, and collected.
     I'm captivated by my gold-coated cuffs,
       their diamond-crusted casings.
         I complain that they're constraining
           but cling to their cold, precious metal,
             clasp them to my wrists until they carve and cut
               my crêpe paper skin as if to coax a confession
                 or challenge conflicting conceptions
                   that I must exist through the ages
                     as either the crooked nosed, capricious crone
                       cackling around the cauldron
                       or as a coy and composed carbon copy
                         marvelling at the sparkling chrome bars of my cages.
                   I marvel at these capable hands
                     reminded of the times they've clawed and climbed,
                     collected dirt beneath my nails,
                       when they've coddled or intertwined to bridge connection.
                 I may recline from time to time to have them cleaned and filed,
               cuticles cut and fingernails lacquered with a coat the colour of carnations.
             But on my palm's padded underside my thumb will always find
           rough and crusted callouses, uncompromising pockets
         of courage crystallised into corrugated stalactites.
     Coarse and constant as I count them in a clockwise rotation.
   I finger them in celebration
 of all the cramped, cordoned-off spaces
that serve as conduits of creation.

Amanda Cohen

Desire

A devious
deviant
desire
burns
under
the moonlight
.

the odour
of
night jasmine
enticing
a golden sky
.

she
untamed
wild
animal
yield
her
deepest
a
r
d
o
u
r
.

a dainty
red dress   lifted
on the edge   of lust

.

a drenched
dancing   tongue
delighting
in her
dew

.

fingers   dipped
in moisture
diving into
her sacred

.

.

.

Daiane Moret

Exceptional

Early evening
I enter a charming eatery to dine
seeking some alone time to edit a poem of mine
without intent I end up eavesdropping
on an enamoured enclave of eclectic women
a gathering of great tradition emanates
voices escalate as stories are shared with ease
anecdotes, expertise exclaimed
everything's discussed from the excruciating unjust
to exquisite erotic encounters
that make me blush.

Engaged in electrifying exchange
they listen intently
while exhorting advice, encouragement
and emotional healing in equal measures
entranced, words echo in my ears
as I dissolve into my own thoughts
dipped in their elixir
gripped by a symphony of emotions
I can't envision, not easily understood
until epiphany arrives in my mind's eye
eluding to the beauty of the sisterhood.

Eve may have preceded us
but evolution sees our Eden ever flourishing
this garden embodies strong women
from quiet achievers to world leaders
we are evergreen
having earned our right to be here
as equals on this earth
for years history demeaned our existence
eroded our essence, portrayed us as the weaker sex
evidently an enigma, for experience abounds
female wisdom makes the world round.

Mother Nature has entrusted us
with growing generations
not just incubating embryos
ethereal beings, enigmatic women
ensconced on the front line
effectively applying our female bodies and minds
empathy a secret weapon, emancipation our right
liberation may have come with Flower Power
but we are flowers who empower
from delicate petticoats of eloquent etiquette
to powerhouses in trousers in our element.

Ever so swiftly I'm enveloped
by the enchanting women I was earwigging earlier
engulfed in their ether
encased in the safety of their warm embrace
they elevate my spirit, alleviate my pain
you see we are lucky
we've been embellished with emotional intelligence
and insights of expert spies
we're envoys deployed to enhance, enrich lives
let us bask in the light of our enlightenment
for without exception, women are exceptional.

Erica Hacker

Frankincense

I was five when
my first anxiety flared;
face in the folds
of my grandmother's frock;
I needed to flee,
flee the fear that lurked
four layers below my skin
struggling to find
a way out of the fortress
that was the church

Brown pews, beige walls,
even the stained-glass
windows muted;
humans, packed and breathing,
the air thick with incense
and hypocrisy

Claustrophobia
induced fainting
I figured as I grew older,
but looking back it was
fables floating on incense,
word of the Father
preaching original sin,
women as prostitutes,
fornicators,
the feminine subservient
to her fellow man

My body might have been five,
but my ancient soul flailed
against the falsehoods,
that men had dominion,
over the earth,
the water,
the trees,
and women

It took me years to know
that we are never not broken

You can try to break us now
but you cannot break that
which already is

And our power lies in
not needing to be fixed

Tanya Southey

Girl Guidelines

Grind gutsy goals
Graciously
Guard against garrulous
Gossipers
Gather goofy sniggering
Giggles
Grasp digestible gratitude
Graphically
Guzzle gullible guilt
Gallantly
Galvanise guaranteed goodness
Generously
Grieve intergenerational
Gentrification
Glimpse glimmering forgotten
Galaxies.

Gabrielle Journey Jones

HA

Dear Letter H,
It has been an honour
hearing your history
and how it weaves itself
into your whakapapa
rooted in the 'HA'
the Sacred Breath.

I have spent hours
reading through archives
hemming histories
like a tailor-maid
tracing the heroics
of our femme line.
Did you find it hard to unearth
the histories of heroic women
like Hineahuone, Hinetitama, Hinenui-te-po?
Knowing your womb wove you to her sacred line?
Who knew unearthing her would require looking within,
I mean really looking within.
It is as if her strength
could be our only mirror
held up to the world
for all to see
us and her
in all of our beauty.

How did you manage to weave
Hine-te-iwaiwa's memoir
into the whariki of your whakapapa?
Handling the harakeke with such humility
holding space for the honore kore
the dishonoured, the unborn,
the miscarried, the stillborn.
The harakeke held with such sacrifice
only a mother's hands could know.
How hard is it to hold on to her history;
'Hinaura wife of Tinirau'
knowing how hard it bites
to leave your own baby behind?

How hard did it make it knowing
courage, honour and survival are
interchangeable?
To leave behind your legacy
with your husband
the one with heavy hands
just like Hinaura
hoping one day your own justice
would be served as swiftly
as Hine-nui-te-po's hunger
snaring his mortality in her snatch
returning you to the 'HA' breath
the Sacred Breath
the Ancestral Breath
returning you to the safety of home
held tightly by spirit

breathe
just breathe
HA
HA
HA!

Janette Hoppe

I

i

id
ide
idea
ideate
ideology
ideologue
~~ideal~~

ii

in my native
tongue, i
is topless: it's lost
its head—a lopped
chıcken or dog
-matıc, runnıng
mındless, *wıld*

iii

in my
native tongue,
i is
sometimes topped with a *fada* [i.e. 'long'] soundíng a sílent
scr[*eee*]am – as ín bean sí [banshee: 'woman spírít'] emíttíng hígh-pítched shríeks

iv

is what i think is needed in our [sk]in-deep
society—a transfusion of truth wouldn't go amiss
in place of this iphone ipad ipod iwatch itv
in[s]ane existence where the i:eyes have it...
blïnking döts ïn the sky, ïn the walls,
on the ceïlïng, vïa satellïte & sïrï or alex[ï]
& strangers can link to conversations
you've had in the [quasi¿] privacy of your
very own mani[in]fested ïclouded home

ic [*sic*]
is what i'd intimate is missing in this in[v]erted
semi-[un]conscious, icecap-melting, species-oblit[era]ting
p[last]ic-proliferating, media-misap[prop]riating, ideate-[in]filtrating
p[rot]ectïonïst state where independent id is ımpaired,
Gaia's spirit is shríekíng & ic: to *care intensively* is
the impasse between i-centric conservation &
an[nıhıl]ation

Anne Casey

Jewgirl Juju

Just a perfect girl
with jet-black hair
my parents' jackpot
Joanne they chose
for 'Gracious is Jehovah'
named to be
a four-leafed clover.

Jutted up to be
jolly tall
'juvenile jailbait'
I heard them call.

Jibed about
my Jewish nose
but kept it giant,
never to be
beauty-reliant.

Jostled for joy –
the kind boys jingled –
a jazzy
jubilance
just for being.

Jangled at the end of
locker room jokes
that kept me
jittery
jumpy
my journeys
jerky.

Joined
the fight for justice
for our gender –
(the junket jimmied
for jocks-with-cocks)
and jobs-for-gents-with-no-v'jinas

Juggled the juggernaut of
motherhood
(as belly became jelly)
a jumble of joy &
Jesus-Christ-just-let-me-out-this-jail.

Jammed my dreams
and did the job
janitor to juniors
(just for 18 years).

Now in the jetsam
of a jillion jotted journals
my jaw grown sore from
juxtaposing junk food &
'does my butt jut?' judgements

I've jettisoned the jealousies
along the jagged edge
of 'yes' and 'please'
outstripped the jibber-jabber
and jargon
of being
someone else's bargain.

Now grown juicy
jungled
with Jewgirl juju
I am a menopausal
Jezebel
bejewelled and jangly
I've out-bled
that fibroid-riddled uterus
(never mind the sneeze-and-piss stunt)
finally
it's a damn fine free cunt.

Jumpstarted by
the broken-hearted
I am a jigsaw of
jollification
a jukebox
of juvenescence
a junkie of
gentleness
beyond justification
for my liberation

never again
to jeopardise
the heart-winged
jacaranda tree
the wild-woman jubilee
the jewelweed
jamboree
that is
just me.

Joanne Fedler

Plosives and Explosives Are Coded in Its Sound

K is for Kwik Kopy, it's a hard 'C' sound
It's the clash of castanets
It's the screechy unmarried older sister
In Padua, Kate the so-called shrew
Worn down by that rude man for a bet
But true to herself, until the end
When she suddenly capitulates.
K is queenly and attention-getting
Sure, she has a temper
But look what the K did for the writer of Harry Potter
Who, without a middle initial or name,
borrowed it from her own grandmother, Kathleen, on the advice of her publisher!
K is the wondrous Sri Lankan
karapincha curry leaf
Which Americans have recently discovered is a superfood.
(All good.)
K is Ka, the sinuous unravelling snake
in the *Jungle Book*
And – speaking of kids' books –
Did you know there was a sequel to the *101 Dalmatians*? In that, a fashion line
'Klothes that Klank' was designed by Cruella de Ville, who was out of work
After the Dalmatians put paid to the fur farm she had planned.
A little night music in German would just not be the same – think of it!
No *Klein*, and no *Musik*!

The Muppet Show would have a lonely Kermit: a hermit, a Coleridgean eremite
K sounds like the q in *Requiem For Doomed Youth* – remember? 'The stutter of the machine-guns' rapid rattle'!
K is for Kryptonite, the strong man's weak point.
Plosives and explosives are coded in its sound. Teeth gritted, furniture shaken.
Causing a commotion, expressing emotion
I wondered why the girls in that sonnet by Wilfred Owen were so gentle and passive, and understated, dimmed down and dumbed down and muted
And the harsh and angry sounds were allocated to the weaponry used by boys
That poem is quite dated, cos
K adds staccato snaps and jazz
To shortened forms of words like brekkie
And Trekkie – Captain Kirk, heading the *Enterprise* in his painted-on Lycra pantsuit.
K is the way I blithely express universal acquiescence
in short form:
Compliance with the amoral majority
I agree, it's easy peasy to respond
With this upright letter.
K, I say, on repeat,
Prompted by a request on a faintly glowing screen. All those incoming demands? 'K' shuts them up and shuts them down. Like processed food in a baby's mouth. Dolloped like doses.

Cos, as a woman, it's often expected
That I people please, and – even at times – perhaps act the tease
Consent should surely be
spelled with a K.
It's not easy being green or pristine
Or too clever, by half.
Ursula Le Guin has a K in her name too
It stands for Kroeber, did you know?
JFK needed the last letter of his initials to be forceful. 'JF' would
have surely lacked something, although the K and the family
name it meant did not cover him in that motorcade in Dallas.
K times 3 is those white-robed devils
With their blazing torches and burning crucifixes lynching
those poor peeps
they are not OK with
rounding them up in the (not) OK Corral
K is Kit Kat and kittens and Kwik-Ease
It's the shape of the Kremlin:
like cream puffs made of coloured stone.
It's comfort food full of potassium; and convenient marriages:
empty of compassion, missing Karma, the most crucial ingredient.
It's Kaos, in *Get Smart*,
as opposed to Control.
It's sharp and flaunting and elegant and proud, not like 'smug C'
As Anne Shirley of Avonlea told her teacher friend, who was
'J' of her.

It's Katherine of Aragon, never shamed
Not like young Catherine Howard,
who lost her head
While a stream of her lovers were allowed to be named out loud.
Think of the mother of
all the Kardashians!
How she saved herself precious time spent on embroidering
initials on their hankies by naming them all with the same
letter – what a piece of work!
K is the way I want people I dislike to go:
KOd into the multiverse:
See how they spin – headed forcefully into astral realms
In kombievans and repainted ships named variations of
'Karaboudjan'.

All the eternal Krispy Creme donuts whirl and KFC popcorn
chicken sizzles and Kris Kringle is Santa Claus, and exists
In a blaze of Rice Krispies and
world-class *Das Kapital.*
Like Katniss Everdeen in the arena
made by Plutarch Heavensbee
I lose it, and win;
I get klunked in the head,
in a way Kleenex can't fix.
I see Stars
I spiral into the Kaleidoscope spheres
of God and Goddess.

Devika Brendon

Lullaby

La, ly, la, ly, la, ly, la, ly, la, ly, la
Love, lie, love, lie, love, lie, love, lie.

There's a loveliness in the lonely lady
Illuminating love like it was never lacking
Unlearning loathfulness as default language
Labouring her lament into laughter
The lyricist of her lullaby

La, ly, la, ly, la, ly, la, ly

There's a loyalty in the lonely lady
A lavish lifelong luncheon with the self
Lately it's last night's leftovers
Legumes or lasagne
Likely tossed down by
Lattes or lemon water

Listening to littered leaves
Leap across the lawn
Languidly lying on her leathery lounge
Looking for luxury in the little
Like the large interlaced lattice fence on which florals lay
Or low-lit lamps that linger as company
Or a ladybug lurking along her walls

La, ly, la, ly, la, ly, la, ly
There's a level-headed lawyer in the lonely lady
Although her life remains the fishing expedition of the locals
She's really just on long-service leave
Now she's learning the laws and legislation of her life
Litigating, lecturing and at times liaising
With her own learned friend

Lately, the liability leaks through
Little lesions on her heart
but there's no lapse in her logic
Her law books are filled with
Her lifelong learnings on loss and love
Laureate-like

La, ly, la, ly, la, ly, la, ly, la, ly
There's a loveliness in the lonely lady
Not a long-hair, lipstick-stained lips kind of loveliness
Not a lifeless, lacklustre loneliness
A loveliness that lights souls
Living past the limited edition of a lifetime
One of the 'lucky ones' they'll say, 'lordlike', the 'Lord's work'
Leaving her lucrative legacy in the love letters she lived out
A life that will be learnt as laudable long after she leaves

…

Who thought a lonely lady could be this legendary?

La, ly, la, ly, la, ly, la, ly, la ly
Love, lie, love, lie, love, lie, love, lie.

Ruth Fesseha

M for Marie (who'd prefer to be N for naughty and nude)

Mesdames et Messieurs und meine Munchkins,

I LUV IT WHEN YOU CALL ME BIG MOMMA

A Mick?
Yea, that's a mnemonic – Mne-Mo-nic!
Maire ni Murchada is anam dom,*
Meravigliosa Marie,
Minion of Murphy

I LUV IT WHEN YOU CALL ME BIG MOMMA

Not from the Minoan era
Nor a miserly mendicant,
Machiavellian, Michelangelo-ian,
Matisse-ian, Marx-ian,
Macbeth-ian…
Medusa is MY middle name

I LUV IT WHEN YOU CALL ME BIG MOMMA

Marooned …
I've mooched
In Moonee Ponds,
Mordialloc an' Melbourne,
My misanthropic meditations
Missing the Malthusian masses
Until I met Myles Minchin,
Muncho, MUNCHO ammmmore

* Irish for Marie, daughter of Murphy, or Marie Murphy

I LUV IT WHEN HE CALLS ME BIG MOMMA

Maternity made me malade.
Mon Mauriac
Milked and milked,
Munched an' masticated,
With molars immmmmmature,
My mam-ill-ae.
Mastitis?
Merde!

I LUVED IT WHEN HE CALLED ME HIS MOMMA

Now in my middle years,
Meno-pause and many tears,
My menstrual cycle's disappeared,
Vagina's dried up…
So I smmmmmmear
Mashed mango an' masses of melon,
Mascarpone à la moutarde
On MY mons Mont-Parnassian,
Making multiple orgasimmmmms
As Myles mounts me

I LUV IT WHEN HE CALLS ME BIG MOMMA

An' I'm thinkin' of
Milton, Moliere, De Maupassant,
Marcel Marceau, Mou Mou
An' Marilyn Monroe

While round MY mulberry bush
Multitudes of
Mice and Men
Miao and meander in the mist
As my mate Monty,
Monk from Montenegro,
Manacles me, malevolently,
(Like a Sade-ian Marquis)
And I sucummmmmmb
Mas-o-chis-tically,

I LUV IT WHEN HE CALLS ME BIG MOMMA

But when the
mignon
Monsieur Emmmmmmmanuel Macron
Mesmerises meeeee,
I'll mull *mit mein* MÖET,
Murmuring

'Maybe, Maybe, Maybe'

I'LL LUV IT WHEN HE'LL CALL ME BIG MOMMA

MAIS OUI
   – – –

With thanks to
The Notorious B.I.G. – Big Poppa (Official Music Video)

Marie McMillan

The New Nude

Naked nineteen months postnatal
nowadays the norm is neglect, not nurture.

Prenatal I moisturised myself
nourished the nest and
naively I tried the new aged
and the new fangled.
Self-care was easy
when there was a second soul
within these walls.

I notice my inner narrator
navigating this new terrain.
A narcissist it nitpicks
this continent of flesh
and the blood and bones
beneath it.

Noxiously it notices the 'negatives'
and questions what's normal.
From toenails to nose
it nastily nicknames my ankles cankles.
It ignores these knees that
have knelt to my every need.
Lacking nationalism
it makes me nauseous
circumnavigating the sagginess of my skin
around my navel –
the nucleus that connected me
to yet another next of kin.

It doesn't acknowledge that these nipples
have nurtured my newborn with nectar
but noisily makes niggling remarks about
their nonconformist decline from north.

Nonetheless, I note there is neutral ground.
In nothingness I find the 'now'
that pulls me back to the present and
the neurotic noise I name Ego
no longer leads.

Between the nine-to-five,
nappies changes and nursery rhythms
I gently begin to give gratitude
to this magnificent vessel.

I let go of nostalgia and allow myself
to revel in neck nuzzling by my lover.
Reigniting nuptials to have and to hold in a new way
and noticing the nuances between tender touches
in niches that no longer feel the same.

I begin to embrace myself with these arms
that have nursed my child
throughout sleepless nights
while she nods off.

A novice in this new role
I take baby steps
in sitting with my nemesis
whilst seeing myself nude.

Stacey Cotter Manière

Who showed you how to feel good?

let there be / lavender /
silvering over seams / done with
noxious zones / here's to folks who
long for rapture & do not think themselves
obscure / so / only the offered / prior /
cognisant / wholehearted / a leaf asking for the
light / a pearl without onus to swallow / your butch
dog, offering its belly to incoming comrades before
even crossing the threshold / here's to rolling open in the
doorway / we are throwing invocations all the time / can
we touch / in opaque tentative ways? / originate here, home
/ glory / it opens through eavesdropping on the nervous
'yes' / safe / so welcome the earnest 'yes!' / shame / less /
I hover, candle-lit, coveting the hollered 'YES' from those
who know badder / who showed you how to feel good? /
(I've) come / (at) home / lips open, hands
of glitter, hips rolling water,
/ a poster at the oceanaut stroll:
'onanism not ownerism' / some of us buy our dicks
& some of us possess countless / knuckled to
fibres that feed & hold & fold in / kiss you
with this royal wave / consider the
obelisk, the oscillating /
oh / oh / oval

Rowan Rose

Dear Letter P

Dear letter P
You have let us down
With your prison of patriarchy, patriotism and policing
Give us passion, people power and peace
Give us poetry

Give us popcorn and poppy petals
Passion fruit and paper planes
Please pass me the peculiar
Pleasure me with perfect precision

You can keep your prim and proper
Your prom queens and kings and princesses
Prepare for the people's revolution cause it's here
Price that on your parking pay machine

Let's pay it forward to the precious
To the players waiting to be picked
Let's pray for the persecuted pencils that stopped professing
Let's protest the privilege that pervades our public system

Give us pride without the prejudice
A president who's not a prick
Protect us from polite politics
Passive aggression perpetuates what's sick

Pave the way for the people's performance
Void of promise of a pretty paradise
No more push or pull please
Present us with a parallel paradigm

Polly has put the kettle on
She's got the pressure at boiling point
The patriarchy no longer polarises the people
We are privy to its pretence and perversion

So dear letter P
I offer you my presence
This pussy is a poet
And I have spoken

Miriam Hechtman

Quick to quote me as queen

In the quiver on my back, a batch of arrows quiver;
questions weighing heavy:
if my body doesn't show
my genderless quintessence,
how do I explain this quality?

Quiet queen inside my body one day,
quiet king comes quickly next.
My body isn't static,
my body is a quest.

On my back the arrows question still,
with arrowheads of quarts,
a quartet of semiquavers,
quickening my heart.

Bow bracing at the ready, just in case somebody asks,
I'll tell them, 'yes, my questions burn',
and shoot one to the stars.

So quietly I'll lighten this quarry of a heart,
and release my inner quarrelling
to some less querulous God.

Be still, quixotic mind who seeks to solve what should be left,
be with me genderless quintessence,
restful inner nest.

Queen and King, ungendered jester, everything I may be,
whichever one shows up today
won't define my quality.

Boy Renaissance

Eternally Persistent

Reluctant with restraint and
Rampant with remorse
I regurgitate in to life
Resurrected in a ruthless
Resemblance of a man

Resuscitated by the rhapsody of this rapture
I restore my resolve to remember
The reckless robbery of my repudiation and
Resist the request to rescue
by the redeeming right to rise
Reviling, the river is me.

Rippling and rippling
I take refuge in reinstating rafters
With the Raven song reverberating
I return, I redeem, I recover
The ravine is holding me.

And there I retrieve my remains
From roadsides of Rosemary and Redwood
In reverence radiating rays
of Rejuvenating Relationships with all
Reclaiming the rudimentary riddle
of who
am I.

Andrijana Miler

Sound

      There's a sound   I can't quite make out

            (whisper)

                        (hissss)

(hush)

      rustling pages / sweeping pen

shhk shhk: shuttle and loom
steady ssssss: spinning wheel
spaces of solitude
         (where we have known ourselves)

     What sounds like suburban stability?
shuffling simulations of servitude / shrunk to the spectacle of
serving you
following scripts laid out for us: sobbing at
soapies / shrieking
      scavengers at sensational sales:
always squabbling over scraps
         (this is how you have known us)

This sound
is sometimes
silence.

the silence of sisters who went missing   the silence of sisters
for whom we prayed   sisters who reappeared in headlines
the next day having been found guilty   of saying no   in
6,500 languages and still   not being heard.

straps tighten she stutters searches for safe-words there
are no safe words   every sound uttered = life sentence
  sinner

        spinster   sheila

slut

        screaming sirens   still night
          someone   gasps

s.   t.   o.   p

……………ssssstatic   between radio stations…………

our funerals   lesser news   than sport

What sound shrugs free of selective.page.bound history –
) This (
is how we shall know ourselves:

sigh

        shimmer

                swell   soar

scatter strike

                scourge   storm.

        slide   slip

                       soothe sting

                resound.

                      sustain.

                       survive

sing

Sarah Temporal

Tuesday's Still Life

Tis 5.30 when I throw open the fridge and
two previously opened, fractionally emptied chicken stock cartons fall
like dominoes onto the tiles.
Tired, I traipse toward the sink and thrash inside its torso to find a sponge.
Tiles cleaned, I tackle the task of tea.
What to eat?
Traumatised chops, left over from last Tuesday
forgotten behind opened tins of tomato.

Terrific!

Tea planned and table spread; together we sit to talk about our day.

Today Master T stayed inside due to the torrential rain and was tormented by Thomas whose tally of merits towered over HIS. Alternatively, HIS toastie from the tuck shop was a spectacular treat.

Terrific! I tell him.

Then I take another tipple from my Tempranillo and settle in to listen to the animated Miss T
tell me her Shakespearean tragedy.

Today totally sucked! Tanya trespassed on HER table and took HER note for Teagan and
criticised HER about its contents.
Triggered I retort, 'She is tantamount to a tool!'
'Tomorrow will be better!'

She agrees, and triumphantly I turn to transfer the emptied plates to the turgid, detergent tumble.

'Time for the bath,' I state.
They tumble in along with a truckload of bubbles, whilst Treacle, the cat, traverses the tub.
'Two minutes,' I tell them (as I secretly watch traces of dirt tremble and fall off their flanneletted faces).
'Time to get out.'
Towels at the ready, they torpedo out of the tub and torment me with their shouts.

Teeth cleaned and cotton T-shirt nighties on,
I suggest that it's time for bed.
NOT YET, they trill.
My patience abating. 'TIME FOR BED!' I restate.
'BEFORE I TERMINATE THE INTERNET!'
Thwarted they take to the task.

Tenderly now, my voice tempered, I tuck them in tightly and torture their cheeks with too many kisses.
I turn to tip toe out of the room and silently say,
'*BonneNuit*, night, night,' as I witness tired eyes closing.

Task complete, I transform back into untethered me
and treasonously treble,

Terrific!

Now, where's my Tempranillo?

Ginette Ball

Uterus

Unadulterated

undying
umbilical love
wrapped around unfaithful, uninspired, and unjust upstarts.

She is but an unconscious and at times, unruly vessel
to carry our unscrupulous names

to be used and abused

her only utility.

You tear her apart
to unpack her unearthly parts
to try and understand this complex
unhinged brain
the unrelenting emotions
the unbridled hormones
the unnerving rage unleashed at all this undermining by you
and your unworthy sons.

How very unattractive
her uterus makes her
how very unfeminine
when the hysteria takes her.

So ugly, how opinionated she can be.
'Maybe she needs a hysterectomy.'
Maybe she just needs to be taken
SERIOUSLY.
And I bet you thought this would be
an angry poem
and it probably was
and hell, it probably should be
but the truth is
she's so much more
than how he writes her
in his story.

She is
the universe untold
a secret; undisclosed
a mystery; unsolved
despite all your unrelenting efforts
to un-robe her

She is
an empire of compassion; unconquered
every uncharted curve and contour;
coordinates of unprecedented understanding
like a composer reads his music
bringing the symphony alight
only a woman can read love into life
like the unequivocal poetry she is,

make it dance in your eyes
like bubbles in wine; unforgettable
give it a way
without a thought
without a question; unconditional.

The buttons of her uncontainable beauty undone to make way for you,
She unearths the undeserving
She enshrines the unborn.
So that not even the sound of unabashed scorn from a husband can be felt by the spawn inside.

Despite the unforgiving world
bringing her to her knees
despite the birth pangs
every unsolicited scream
every unbearable squeeze
she continues to bloom
unapologetically.
Her silk still takes the shape of your unatoned hurt
as your head meets her unflinching chest.
For there is no greater rest
than this unsurpassed sanctum of serenity
than this unashamed, unparalleled, unworldly uterus.

Rana Salem

To the Earth, Love V

Voluminous vegetation your gift to the vulnerable
in return you received volumes of vortex vomit
from vultures filling a void,
a species of victim vindictive vermin
vouching vociferates virtues from vile voices
vibrating demonstrations of uninvited visitation
visual greed the vivacious need to vitiate
represented by vigilant actions to reduce vegetation.
While nasty vernacular continues to vilify Indigenous villagers
historically venereal vengeance on vaginas was perceived as valour
is now deconstructed like a venetian blind with a vendetta for vengeance,
and on the verge of a verdict by visually exploding volcanoes
still the greedy vipers violate
and their only vice is to veto veracity
while continuously exposing violent attitudes towards vintage virgins.

Mother Earth please know,
we are not all vampires vanquished to vandal
with vigour we strum violins in your vineyards
we value your versatility and vast vicinity
visualising visionary vital vitality
and as we vanquish vase-line over veneer
we don't need to sleep with the enemy or be their valentine
as us the venerable vagabonds do what is vital
by demanding miners to vacate
for the vagary of the environmental vein
our vantage point is the evidence drawn from validity
because we understand variables to verify the raw and valuable
by virtue, we will remain valiant as we express gratitude
for your sharing of your vastness.

Vanessa S. Lee-AhMat

Women's Eyes

As I wander this world
With my woman's eyes
I witness life beyond its disguise
And become weary
At the place which we've arrived
Where greed
Has spun a communal demise

As I wander this world
With my woman's eyes
I see how whims
Have warped and wounded
Through misplaced pride
And I wish for wisdom watershed
To be rewoke and revived

As I wander this world
With my woman's eyes
I look out of the window and into the wild
I welcome the wonder
Of this watchful night
And the hopeful wishes
Of nature's dying light

Ella Mitchell

Ex Tempore

You're so extra!
Let me explicate –
you exhale words,
expelling steam like an overheated espresso machine,
your exhortations hiss and gurgle,
you rush to expel them,
expunging your demons with the force of poetry.
Your words extol, exclaim, examine.
Expletives explode like bombshells
as you exult in your extraordinary lexicon.

I wait, expectant, for you to
extricate yourself from your exoskeleton of words,
expose your exquisite self, expedite your existence
from earthbound to existential.
I long to make our words expand like wings,
so we can soar like extraterrestrial beings
above the excrement of this dull world,
expose the exosphere created by our words,
exchange vowels and consonants instead of rings
to execute our wordy union.

Such mental exercise is all I crave.
We would make ourselves exceptions to the rules of all but grammar,
exemplars of verbal exploration, our tongues twisting in admiration.
You excuse yourself, claiming exemption from emotion,
your devotion to words your only exemplar.

My vision dashed, my wings clipped, I return to earth.
With the power of my words, I exorcise you from my being,
I expel you from my heart, I expurgate you from my soul.
I exult that, without you, my horizons will expand,
I watch you extinguish, fading behind me,
as I write a new poem, exuberant that
I can expel all mention of you, my EX!

Lou Steer

I Used To Ask Y

I used to ask Y about everything
I used to say yes to everyone
But I think my youth is leaving me
And now, you are leaving me too

I used to yearn for everything
I used to yield to everyone
But yesterday was years ago
So why not break every yoke with you?

I used to ask Y about everything
I used to be young for everyone
Now I yawn and yell at the stars
I'm too tired to ask why about you

Jessica Chapnik Kahn

Layers of Z

Scattergories in the pub.
When we froze on Z, he asked,

'Why last?
I mean.
Why IS Z last?'

'Well, She wasn't always Last.'
I zapped.

'You see,
Zed, AKA Zee,
Has a survival instinct in her HER story.

A Roman man once gave her the boot.
He kicked her from the dictionary.
Kaput.

Prior to the Latin alphabet, she was the Greek letter Zeta.
And like her name suggests, quite a mesmerising Diva.

A layer before Zeta, she was the Hebrew letter *Zayin*.

The seventh letter with the crown,
That's how they called her all around.

She was dazzling, she was strong,

Jeez.
It all went wrong.

You see,

In ancient Hebrew, killing weapons are named *Zayin*.
Should have seen it comin'.

In modern Hebrew, the penis is named *Zayin*.
Connotations firing and rewiring.

That was the beginning of the end.
Zayin now means – "fucking bad".

Zayin also stands for "Hell, no."

So,
Hell, No!

Using your *Zayin* as a sword,
Means that now you zip and we talk.

ZAYIN.

You cannot kill us softly,
You cannot hide the body.

We see you and we're telling,
We DRAW the line and HERE IT's END-ING.

ZAYIN.

We are claiming back the letter,
Mend the world and make it better.

With a Buzz and lots of noiZe,
Back on Dictionary Avenue, she has poise!

She seized her way and no longer redundant
She is whizzy, Zesty and oh so mezzo vibrant,

Zayin, Zeta, Zee
She's here to daze, she's here to Be.'

*

I realised there was silence in the pub.
People surrounded us and clapped.

I had the stage.
The rage.

'Total poli-ti-ci-Zation,'
A dictionary can turn into a war zone location.

Us sisters,
We stand by each other.

Each letter supports another

From queen A to heroine Zed,

We are the Amazons
of the Alphabet.

Limor Fayena

About the Authors

Anna Forsyth is an editor, poet and event manager. In 2014, she founded Girls on Key, a feminist poetry organisation that hosts poetry readings for women and gender diverse poets. Her poems have appeared in journals in print and online including *FourW, Poetry New Zealand, Landfall, Not Very Quiet* and *Baby Teeth*. Her collections of poetry are *A Tender Moment Between Strangers* and *Beatific Toast*. She was the joint winner of the NAIDOC Red Room poetry prize 2018. She was the publishing manager and editor of Girls on Key Press.

Bina Hammer is a full-time student, part-time photographer and occasional writer. She lives in Sydney with her grandparents.

Amanda Cohen is an American writer living between Sydney and New York. Her poetry pushes the limits of vulnerability, drawing both tears and laughter from audiences in Australia and in pockets across the globe. She has featured at several literary events including the Sydney Poetry Lounge, Kings Cross Theatre and Poetica.

Daiane Moret is a spoken-word poet and artist. Her work navigates personal experiences while deconstructing given identities. Brazilian roots paint the narrative as she retells stories, resignifying herself through them. She has featured at Poetica, Sydney Writers' Festival, National Reconciliation Week, Newcastle Fringe Festival and Melbourne Spoken Word Festival.

Erica Hacker is an emerging force on the Sydney spoken-word poetry scene, bringing a unique style and big emotions to the stage. She's worked in the performing arts for many years, including head of marketing roles at Word Travels, Seymour Centre and Sydney Dance Company.

Tanya Southey is a people collector, tea drinker, dog lover, poetry junkie and a published author. Her children's adventure story *Ollie and the Starchaser* subtly explores grief and loss. In 2018, Tanya completed a poetry challenge – #52words52weeks – where she collaborated with London street photographer Denise Smith to create a poem a week. This project was published as a coffee table book *StreetWise* late last year. They enjoyed 2018 so much they have continued their weekly connection for three years, never missing a week in the 156 consecutive weeks that followed. Tanya's mission, whether in writing or work, remains to help people reach their full potential.

Gabrielle Journey Jones is a poet, percussionist and community builder living on Yuin Country, Far South Coast NSW. She has established ongoing projects including Creative Womyn Down Under (2006), Poetic Percussion (2018), and Writing Open Mic Bega 'WOMB' (2021). Gabrielle has shared her spoken word performances as feature poet at local, national and international events for over twenty years. Her collections *Spoken Medicine* (2017) and *Etymology of Courage* (2021) have been published by Ginninderra Press.

Janette Hoppe's poetry reflects her New Zealand Maori and Australian heritage. She is the creator of Papatuanuku Press, an indie publication that oversees the Women of Words project; the Blue Series and Blue Youth Series projects; and the Poetry Bomb.

Anne Casey is a Sydney-based award-winning Irish poet/writer and author of four collections – *where the lost things go* (Salmon Poetry 2017), *out of emptied cups* (Salmon Poetry 2019), *Portrait of a Woman Walking Home* (Recent Work Press 2021) and *the light we cannot see* (Salmon Poetry 2021). A journalist, magazine editor, legal author and media communications director for thirty years, her work is widely published internationally and ranks in *The Irish Times*' Most Read.

Joanne Fedler is an internationally bestselling author of thirteen books, writing mentor and women's rights activist. She runs writing workshops and has online writing courses for aspiring authors including Writing As Medicine for the Soul on Insight Timer. Her book *Things Without a Name* has been optioned for a six-part TV series.

Devika Brendon's poetry and short stories have been published in Australia, India, Italy, Africa and Sri Lanka. Devika is an academic, editor, reviewer and columnist. She was awarded the Henry Lawson Prize for Poetry and the Adrian Consett Stephen Prize for Prose at the University of Sydney. She is currently consultant content editor for the SEALA Network and content editor for the *New Ceylon Writing Literary Journal* (established in 1970). Devika was consultant editor for *Fern Asia* magazine and a poetry editor for Girls on Key Publishing in 2020–21.

Ruth Fesseha is a lawyer and consultant by day and a creative spoken-word poet by night, having performed at numerous events around Sydney, from the Bankstown Poetry Slam, to Shalom's Moth evening, the Women Writes Movement, Afrikapital Slam and Jam, the Women of Diversity Dinner and even at NSW Parliament House. Ruth's spoken-word poetry journey developed at the intersection of her love for singing, writing and storytelling.

Marie McMillan, from Dublin, has been described as a spoken- word performer (who tends towards self-deprecating, satirical humour) and has given readings of her work at the Woollahra, Newcastle and Sydney Writers' Festivals, Woollahra Poets' Picnic, the Tasmanian Poetry Festival, Seniors Got Talent and Joycean Bloomsday events. Several of her poems and short stories have won or been placed in Australian and overseas competitions. *The Lost Day*, her debut novel about drink spiking, was published by Europe Books UK in the London spring of 2021.

Stacey Cotter Manière is a poet and creative director recently relocated to Sydney from Paris. She enjoys storytelling across various mediums and the cross-pollination that happens as a result. Stacey has been published in *The Artisans* (France), *The Lissome Magazine* and in the anthology *SMEAR – Poems for Girls* published by Andrews McMeel Publishing.

Rowan Rose is interested in change and the many ways that living things interact with change. They give thanks to all the queers, artists and activists who have taught them.

Miriam Hechtman is founder and curator of *The Alphabet of Women*. She is an Australian writer, poet and creative producer and the founder and host of Poetica, a live poetry and music initiative in Sydney. She is co-presenter and producer of Wordsmith – the poetry podcast, and one-half of the poetry duo fourlinesproject.

Boy Renaissance is an AFAB non-binary poet and spoken-word artist. They are honoured to be representing their unique angle of womanhood in this publication.

Andrijana Miler is a Bosnian-born multidisciplinary artist exploring a panoply of creative practices focused on human identity, (dis)connection to nature and mental healthcare. Currently working as a psychosomatic counselling practitioner in Sydney, she continues deepening her art practice though performing her music and poetry, exhibiting her photography, and attending various talk panels, focused on the experience of exile, refugees and cross-cultural mental health practices in Australia. Part of her life story was documented in ABC Radio National's program *Stamp of war – the end of Yugoslavia*.

Sarah Temporal is a prize-winning performance poet, writer and educator. Her work has been published in the *Australian Poetry Anthology* and was highly commended in the XYZ Prize for Innovation in Spoken Word. Sarah runs Poets Out Loud, a community arts initiative based in the Northern Rivers NSW, and is soon to release her debut poetry collection.

Ginette Ball is a teacher, writer and poet who holds both a Bachelor of Arts degree and a Masters of Education from Sydney University. She regularly shares her poetry at Poetica and has helped run the night since its launch in 2017. Ginette has contributed her poetry to several online platforms and was a feature storyteller at the Mama Creatives' Story Slam in 2018 and a feature poet at Sydney Jewish Writers Festival in 2019

Affectionately known as 'Jacque the melancholic' among friends, **Rana Salem**, aka The Poet's Daughter, is a mental health social worker, wistfully obsessed with the human condition. Her poetry is infused with coffee, loneliness and other common postmodern addictions.

Vanessa S. Lee-AhMat is from the Yupungathi and Meriam people, Cape York and the Torres Strait. Vanessa is a poet, writer, published author, a social epidemiologist and a cultural broker. She has performed her poetry at the Sydney Writers' Festival and more recently was a producer with the Unspoken Word poetry project. Vanessa has been an invited panellist with the Sydney Festival of Dangerous Ideas and has worked with a choreographer from NASIDA to turn one of her poems into a seven-minute dance performance. Vanessa's poetry publication *Cockatoos in the Mangroves* was published in September 2020.

Ella Mitchell is a Melbourne-based creative producer, a writer, poet, photographer and filmmaker. She is one-half of the poetry duo fourlinesproject.

Lou Steer is a cabaret poetry diva, performing her original poetry in museums, nightclubs, festivals and even graveyards since 2010. She speaks of fractured hearts and thorny roses. Lou's poems are widely published and anthologised. She convened the slam poetry event Caravan Slam for three years.

Jessica Chapnik Kahn is an Argentinian-Australian singer-songwriter, actor and writer. She has worked in theatre and TV, played in the bands of some of Australia's finest artists, and released two solo albums under the moniker Appleonia. She is the author of children's book *Lenny and the Ants* and poetry collection *MADRE,* and co-author of the biography *A Repurposed Life.*

Limor Fayena is a software engineer, a film lecturer and an MS warrior. Limor holds a BFA in Film and Television. She writes about cinema, feminism, and politics. Limor is a Sydneysider who arrived in Australia from Israel in 2006.

Acknowledgements

I first want to acknowledge the lands of the Gadigal people of the Eora Nation who traditionally lived on the Sydney coast in Australia where this book was conceived and edited, this precious land where I live, work and raise my daughters. This book has been written on many lands. I want to honour those lands, the nature on those lands, and the First Nations women of those lands.

The Alphabet of Women holds so many stories and I am forever grateful to each woman who jumped on board and ran with their letter. Your trust in this process, your willingness to share so deeply about your own woman story is so very much appreciated.

There are many people who have brought this book to fruition. In a way, every woman, be it friend or stranger, who has travelled along my path has been inspiration for this anthology. From my Artist's Way tribe way back in the noughties to all the writers, poets, musicians, artists and teachers I have met throughout my life, so many women have walked beside me. To my dear friend Bianca for light-heartedly suggesting I write the whole alphabet. To Karen, Karima, Maureen and Clair, my earthly guides who open the doors to what lies above and beneath. To my women's group, for mirroring to me all that is. To Ella for Fourlines and fierce friendship. To Jane at Gertrude and Alice Bookstore for opening the shop to Poetica and laying the foundations for all that has followed. And for your friendship. To the Poetica community, especially my dear friend Gin. What a bunch of good folk. I always knew my tribe was out there. Thank you for showing up. To Kelly van Nelson for jumping on the mic with me and starting our poetry podcast *Wordsmith*. To Stephen Matthews and the team at Ginninderra Press for taking on this creative beast! To Grace Felstead for your absolute care and intuition designing the cover. To Ione Skye for your tender foreword and support of this book. To Eliza Scott and Emma Harris for bringing this book to life for the stage. Your artistry and vision shed new light on these stories.

To my Nana Resi for holding words and writing me birthday poems and love letters and keeping all my words neatly filed away in your cupboard. To Marsha, for being such a supportive and encouraging mother-in-law and a poet too. To my sisters Natalie and Leah, the sisterhood runs deep and I am buoyed by our shared history and future. To my dad Aaron, for introducing me to poetry greats Leonard Cohen and Allen Ginsberg, and for sharing your own poetry with me. I treasure you and it all. To my mum Dora for reading every word I have ever asked you to read and for your unconditional love and guidance. You have taught me so much and I love you.

To Guy, thank you for your unwavering support for all that I do and for all who I am. And to my Noa and Lina – my sky and earth. You three are my little universe. No words. Just love.

www.ingramcontent.com/pod-product-compliance
Lightning Source LLC
Chambersburg PA
CBHW062153100526
44589CB00014B/1820